Wild Raspberries

Wild Raspberries

Beth Paulson

Plain View Press
P. O. 42255
Austin, TX 78704

plainviewpress.net
sb@plainviewpress.net
1-512-441-2452

ISBN: 978-0-9819731-2-8
Library of Congress Number: 2009923771000

Cover art: *Walk Your Heart*, mixed media, © Ann Dettmer, 2008

Acknowledgements

Grateful acknowledgments are made to the following publications where these poems first appeared:

"Mallards" and "The Color of Snow" (nominated for the 2009 Pushcart Prize) in *Aurorean*; "Grandfather's Magic" in *Advocate*; "Weather at 12,000 Feet" (First Prize 2006) in *Blind Man's Rainbow*; "Quantum Theory of Lilacs" and "Wild Raspberries" in *Blueline*; "Traditions" in *Heartlodge*; "After," "Life at the Edge" (2007 Mark Fischer Prize Runner Up) and "Love Geology" in *Innisfree*; "First Waves" in *Iris Magazine*; "Flag Woman" and "Wild Grace" in *Mountain Gazette*; "Rattlesnake" in *Pegasus*; "Night Walk" in *Plainsongs*; "Like God," "Consider" and "When I Knew They Were Gone" in *Poetry for the Spirit*; "Return" and "The Country of Rain" in *Red Owl*; "September Yellow" in *Ruah*; "First Words," "Looking Back" and "To the Young Doctor" in *Shemom*; "Eagle Lake," "October Night" and "Ten Things About a Piano" in *Slow Trains*; "After That Day" in *Still Crazy*; "Day Planner," "Hollyhocks" (nominated for the 2007 Pushcart Prize), "Hopscotch" and "The Hard Way" in *Sweet Annie and Sweet Pea Review*; "Colliers' Encyclopedia, 1956" in *Tapestries*; "Primroses" and "Red Fox" in *Terrain*; "Moon, Trees, Snow" and "Summer Spell" (2007 Mark Fischer Honorable Mention) in *The Lyric*; "Transition" in *The Oak*; "Eagle" and "Gathering," in *Tributaries*; and "Shoulder Season" in *Voicings from the High Country*.

I am sensual in order to be spiritual.

Mary Oliver

Contents

Love Geology   57

First Words

Hopscotch

In the schoolyard under a mountain
blue day, three girls laugh and chatter,
bright-jeaned legs like new crayolas.

Once down a Kentucky hill
I walked early to play
with other girls of eight or nine,
bare-legged in our cotton skirts.
I'd toss a rock or rabbit's foot
into a numbered space,
then jump in my scuffed oxfords
and bend over to retrieve it,
an inverted arabesque.
Eager voices overlapped the lines
we hopped in turn around,
chalked numbers up to twelve,
pink-cheeked faces shining,
eyes watching each other
aim for the safety of squares
scrawled on frosty asphalt,
counting minutes till the bell rang.

How impossible to imagine
the women we'd become,
leaping through years of lost loves,
marriages, job moves, child raising,
not knowing when we'd lose balance,
lean too far one way and take a fall.

After That Day

One day the teacher
opened a large book;
I sat close enough to see
her slim hands turn the page,
then point right at a word
she said was *Look.*
Tongue behind her teeth,
she showed us how to say
the sound we'd later use
for *love* and *luck* and *lonely.*

Next she sounded the letter *k,*
a whispered clicking in the throat,
then pointed to the *o*'s,
two wide eyes looking at us
first grade children.

Words fell out of every book
I opened after that day—
I carried them home on my lips,
listening for what they might mean,
tasting their sharp, black edges.

Colliers' Encyclopedia, 1956

It was sometime after the rose
Kohler sofa and easy chair
and Bendix automatic washing machine
the encyclopedia salesman came to call.
From the hallway we could see their faces
under the light of the floor lamp,
his papers spread out for signing
on the Formica coffee table.
With installment payments of ten dollars
each month to that book company,
what hopes our parents had for us four girls.

Being firstborn, I learned early
knowledge was a burden—
it took two hands to lift one to my lap—
black volume with few color photos
and so much small print.

Later we'd remember Dad
sitting in his chair at night, tie loose,
turning those weighted pages,
his face afloat in the smoke
of a Camel cigarette, lost to us
somewhere between Aardvark and Zygote.

Grandfather's Magic

Soon as we came inside the door,
he said he had new tricks for us,
pipe in his mouth, face rumpled as his shirt.
Perhaps Grandfather sensed we had too much
realism in the city where we lived.
At his house there was magic.

He'd find a ping-pong ball behind one ear,
from underneath his sleeve, a red silk scarf.
He showed us a black lacquered box
with concealed parts where coins appeared,
then cautioned us to watch his hands
as he laid out a shiny deck of cards.
He made us laugh and wonder at each feat
and gave us hints as we tried to repeat
these simple sleights of hand.

Grandfather had a practical side as well,
a basement workshop where, alone at night,
he built a dollhouse with four rooms, a chest
with secret bottom. Dolls he repaired, too,
and china under the yellow light.

We thought *he* was the magic:
he found our dog when she got lost.
One white Ohio winter he even fixed
the frozen plumbing of our house.

That was why we never could get over
their divorce, how he couldn't mend
a marriage. Love could disappear.

When he moved to an apartment,
he packed away his tools and tricks.
We learned what was illusion, what was true
that year we children grieved,
and when they measured us, how much we grew.

Eagle Lake

In a packed Chevrolet station wagon
we rode there in one day
through Michigan small towns
to cabins clustered by a lake
with a dock and dusty store
pine woods rose up around.
Second from the water's edge,
ours had old linoleum floors,
lumpy sofa, one bathroom,
a kitchen bedrooms opened off.
For two weeks we got up with no clocks.

While our parents fished the cove
or read library books on the front porch,
we girls swam and dove
down to the lake's weedy bottom,
then sunned on the wooden float
with Coppertone and Cokes,
water drops on our warm skin
evaporating into expectant air.

Two blonde boys from Skokie
drove a motorboat we skied behind,
trying to smile like Esther Williams,
knees bent, holding tight the tow rope,
skimming the blue.

Ten Things About a Piano

You're playing the sonata Mozart composed when he was six.

Old music is always stored in the hinged bench.

Other people can play show tunes and sing at the same time.

Winter and Company studio upright, *circa* 1940, dark walnut.

You stopped taking lessons too soon.

Do you remember the name and phone number of the tuner?

You could play all your pieces better if you would practice scales.

An inside wall is the best place for it.

One time when it was moved, it broke its left leg.

Your legs can reach the pedals now.

October Night

Lately I've traveled far
and never left my desk computer,
navigated roads across
the whole United States
over mountain ranges,
across great rivers and lakes
to cities with skyscrapers
and rows of houses.
Looking down like God might
I count trees and vehicles,
saved images from satellites
engineers have hung up in the sky.

With a few finger strokes I'm back
to a two-storey brick house
in a western suburb of Chicago
on a street named Roosevelt
where one October night
Dad, his voice awed and low,
took us out into the dark
back yard to show us Sputnik,
a winking star we strained
to grasp the mathematics of
as we stood watching it race
across black and infinite Space.

First Waves

I carried you, just up from a nap,
        pale, moist hair against my cheek,
from the house over grassy dunes
        and set you on the edge of a continent
where you, timid explorer,
        stepped along the smooth surface
of that strip of shore
        between California and the Pacific.

Your starfish hands open,
        your eyes studied small waves
that lapped cold over our feet
        darkening the plane of sand
we saw our toes sink into,
        then slid in a breath back to the sea.

You laughed from your belly
        and, like a young Columbus,
reached out one arm
        far as it would go—to touch
the salty wind that blew against your face
        or measure the great blue space
where water meets firmament?

With no word yet for *astonished*,
        wide-eyed, you curved your mouth
into a perfect, silent O.

First Words

At low tide the beach extends so far.
　　　　Winter. The rain's stopped
　　　　　　　　and left us this wet, gray sand.
Gulls calling overhead
　　　　swoop to search for dead fish,
light on dark, drenched logs
　　　　rolled onto the strand
by waves long gone, leaving
　　　　behind curved lines of flotsam.

A perfect place to run for you
　　　　in your green jacket,
　　　　　　　　to go far as you can
out toward the great Chinese freighters
　　　　moored in the English Bay
whose sailors in their Mao suits
　　　　ride launches into Vancouver.

We both race far out
　　　　across soft, watery sand
　　　　　　　　our sneakers sink into,
the black ships grow larger,
　　　　you laughing as seagulls screech.

To the Young Doctor

You were so capable at Emergency
      where the paramedics and I
      gave my son to you, bleeding heavy
      from his head one summer morning.

After the bustle of bandages and wheels,
      you touched him like a father would.
I cried though my 12-year-old would not,
      when your needle pulled
      the lines of stitches three times taut,
and all the hour you mended his head
      you told me more than once
      I was not a poor mother.

Beneath dark hair, the scar's still there.

Hollyhocks

Heart-shaped, bright green
leaves, fuzzy and profuse
grow against the south side of the house,
and clustered on the ends of giant stems,
the bright pink, silk-tissue blossoms
of hollyhocks.

Midwestern childhood summers
in my grandparents' garden
I fashioned dolls out of their crinkly blooms
and danced them in my hands
while I stood sundressed and barefoot
in soft, black soil between
the vegetables and railroad tracks.
They were girls I dreamed would travel far.

Five years ago in Colorado
I found hollyhocks again in a gravelly alley
leaning into September, tall and generous.
Resolute, I gathered their seeds,
then planted them like myself
in a dry and rocky place.
I kept hoping we would both take root,
become something
beautiful and new.

Gathering

Return

They weren't waiting for me
but the mountains were
wearing snow against the blue
backdrop of cloudless sky,
their peaks still commanding
the wide and grassy valley.

On their sides the uncountable
pine trees were singing beside
brimming creeks that tumbled
over boulders becoming falls
that plunged and glittered,
and the resolute stone walls
still reflected—here red there silver—
a magnificent shining.

Gathering

Leaving the house
I go out to see

the aspens, for example,
shaking their tenuous green

leaves over the hillside,
swaying on slender white trunks,

their particular shade
limning the dark pines;

and the ragged cottonwoods
resurrected once again

along the full ditch, new-leaved
branches next to those bare,

no longer bearing, holding up
pale limbs like a supplication;

and the wide ribbon of river
unwinding its fast spool

of tan and creamy waters
over gleaming snags and mossy

boulders, humming its loud mantra—
yes yes yes;

and the just-bloomed flax—
their blue petal stars

raised up on the trembling
threads of their stems.

Caution

Cross snowfields one step at a time.
            Go slow. Find purchase
                        in boot prints left by others.
Remember to breathe deep,
            rest when necessary.
Keep your eyes on your feet,
            on each push of heel and toe
                        into the glassy snow.
Above all, don't look down
            the steep you are crossing
and don't rush to the safety
            of mud and shining rock.

When I Knew They Were Gone

A long time ago I believed
each of my small sorrows
made a home in my heart
and stayed there forever.

But that was before
I heard early summer bluebirds
sing to the green valley
from a pine branch,

that was before I looked down
into the scented silk petals
of a just-opened peony,

that was before I drank
water from a high mountain
stream that was snow yesterday.

Iris

The iris are holding up candles
of purple, blue and white,
lighting up the garden another year.
Deer leave them alone,
preferring new-green leaves
of oaks to their sweet scent.

If you look close you see
petals soft and curvilinear
enclose little yellow altars,
how each flower is a tabernacle.

And after hard-fisted wind or long
ropes of rain move through the valley,
iris stand like towers, shining
and even more beautiful.

All my life I wished for
the assurance of roots
and the world said
Wait, Wait, Wait.

Spring Wakas*

1.
So suddenly
the mountain valley
is a haze of new leaves.
Joy infuses
my heart, my body.

2.
Spring wind
shakes budding oak branches
and bends blades of new grass.
I cling to fresh hope
for the world.

3.
I waken to spring
snow blanketing the valley.
May it rest light
on the just-opened
leaves of the aspens.

*Waka is an old Japanese word for a short poem.

Spring Spell

Come to me.
Come like the river so full of itself
        celebrating what's clean and cold.
Come like the rust-colored oak leaves
        unfurling and bursting their buds.
Come like the new grass
        emerging, silken and pliant.
Come like the black she-bear,
        hungering into the valley.
Come like the swallows, violet-green,
        swooping the shimmering air.

After

One early June day we saw the doe
lying under a juniper on a slope.
We'd watched her walk lame the day before.

Some said haul her body out with chains
behind the jeep. Some said bury her,
in dry, rock-filled adobe soil. Meanwhile

we lived a summer near that knoll—
daisies and poppies bloomed and went
to seed and then the hill turned bronze.

In the end we left her where she lay down—
in dying, how many can choose the place?—
her last sensing, fragrant boughs,
last view, immensity.

Quantum Theory of Lilacs

You would think it would be lonely,
this living with so much space
between the stars and us,
between every nucleus
and its electrons. Sometimes
it's a burden knowing how
much room we have to fill with living
inside the uncountable trillions
of atoms our bodies are.

What saves me is the lilac bush,
the one gleaming purple in the noon
sun at the end of the drive,
its heavy-hung clusters of mist
dark lavender yesterday
when sky clouded over.

I like the part of quantum theory
that holds each of us
is made of reassembled parts
of tree or horse or vegetable or flower
like the lilac bush in the light
wind of early summer.

Primroses

At day's end along the dusty path
I saw them, pale-pink votives glowing
      in the gravelly stone
      on the mud bank
      up from the clamoring river.

They were evening primroses
      sprung from gray-green, leathery leaves
      unfolding their silken petals, opening up
      to bright stamen centers.
They were the only blooming in that dark place.

I believe there are people like that, too,
      who cling to what's in this world
      such as the poor person who offers
      the stranger bread or a song.

Life at the Edge

On the surface of the earth
it seems apparent, most action
happens where things meet—
cup to the lip, beak to the nectar,
beetle to the bark, hook to the scales,
dragonfly to the skin of the river.

Slick purple eggplant,
fuzz of ripe peach, bristly pinecone,
silk rose petal that breathes its fragrance
on my fingers—each surface
offers itself to you.

Everything blooms at the edge—
crocus in spring, summer wildflower,
new grass shoots, ancient redwoods.
Great rivers run underground
but on earth's green and blue veneer's
a plenitude of waters.

Half-buried boulder, baby's soft crown,
fur, feather and hair, facial features
of persons I most love—
I'm content with what's exposed,
things that contact, the crusts,
membranes, molecules that cling and cleave,
all open doors and borders.

So I'm grateful skin holds me in,
for fence line, tree line, porch and sky line,
black rim of distant mountain,
white curve of the moon's margin,
and I ponder with a complex brain
a universe in me that has no edge,
no horizon to hold everything inside.

Night Walk

A poem is a walk.
A.R. Ammons

Walk through the hushed fields
beside the nickering horses
past cows resting near a hay barn.

Walk past the river, cool and dark,
humming its night song
between the silent rocks,
between the willowed banks.

Walk beside the shadowed edge
of road that winds through the valley
where house windows wink yellow
beside sheds of forgotten tools.

Count yourself alone
except for cicadas in the trees,
skunks in the brambles,
deer in the deep pines;
except for wild blueberry bushes
along the weedy ditch,
sated black bear crouched in the hills,
and the new moon that touches you
with its mantle of light.

Swan

Up from the dark bank of the green lake
      you carry in your feather basket
          snow dreams,
then speak to me with your black button eyes,
      holding your small head high
          on the slope of your neck
where, nestled in that beautiful curve,
      I am struck by loneliness.

I need something wonderful
      to see today and you come out
          of the cold lake,
      your wings shaking diamonds
          into the broken light.

Rattlesnake

In the filtered light of oaks,
it curled, fat and gleaming,
wearing pale diamonds
over its sleek, green length.
I could not fully understand
its snake language
when it showed me the red spark
of its tongue. But it would not
let me look long at this beauty
and momentary power.

Beside the path up from the creek
I first saw it on a rise
after I heard a warning hiss.
You know how they collect
and can be unleashed—
all our coiled fears—
when you look close at a snake.

Seven Snapshots of a Juniper Tree

i.
You green the hillsides
in summer and your boughs
praise the blue sky.

ii.
I gather your white berries
onto string like a Navajo woman
and make Ghost Beads.

iii.
Fractal and segmented,
your cuttings are lace
on my windowsill in a vase.

iv.
Hiking in July heat,
I rested in the rough shade
of your low branches.

v.
Are you *juniperus*
or *sabina osteosperma?*
While botanists debate this,
I call you *hardy.*

Continued

vi.
Your wood makes sturdy
fence posts, your bark
stripped by the high desert
where you thrive.

vii.
I pluck one pungent berry,
break it open and inhale
a mountain stream.

Summer Spell

Cinquefoil fireweed paintbrush flax
       aster larkspur bluebell vetch
gentian iris lupine phlox
       clover lily bistort sedge:

Wonder what's untamed and spree
       sprung from slope and meadow bed
and rocky stream, a potpourri
       purple, yellow, white and red.

Where elk live and mountain sheep
       golden eagle young first fly
raven and the red-tailed hawk
       bloom in August and July:

Gentian iris lupine phlox
       clover lily bistort sedge
cinquefoil fireweed paintbrush flax
       aster larkspur bluebell vetch.

Day Planner

The goldfinches are already out
feeding under the leafy gambel oak,
making their morning music in the sun's light,
flashing and flickering like fishes,
yellow to black to yellow-green.

Goldfinches do not need to arrange the day.
They know they will be winging
from rosy thistle to black-eyed sunflower
and beaking seeds from the needled earth
under the pine's airy branches
before they rest inside its shelter.

Before Grass

Where did the clouds rest?
      How did the trees?

Was it the secret song of grasshoppers,
      breath of wild horses?
Was it the shadow summer
      lupines cast on a hillside?
A dream of the wind?

When it grew tall and green,
      did grass become the language
of stones? Did it become
      stalks for the rain?

The Country of Rain

For a month it has been raining.
Sometimes hard sheets
pound roof and road.
Other times rain falls soft
as breath on the faces of flowers,
slowly weighting down
the long arms of trees.

Flags of wild grass
undulate in the watery wind,
the brown river overflows its banks,
red earth pours thick
down the sides of sodden hills.

Afternoons the ominous sky fills
with gray cotton, white light flares,
and thunder echoes down valley.

Anchoring

In first dawn igniting the arroyo
       then slow ascending sky

the color of poppies before opening,
       something like happiness
           is possible. Later

you imagine dawn
       in all the shades of green—

dark firs on the steep slopes
       of the cragged peaks
           newly rolled hay,

grass springing from adobe, and
       junipers anchoring the foothills
           with their boughs.

Wild Grace

Every summer the columbines
are so perfect I can hardly believe
their blue and white blossoms
rising up in the high country
from rocky impossible slopes.

At edges of snowfields or
along streambeds, they survive
equally in honeyed sunlight
or under the cold rain's lashes.

But I believe no person
can be so upright all of the time
or kneel before a storm
the way they do.

Their curved blue petals
and white-cupped sepals
hold only a few raindrops:
what can I do with my tears?

Like God

The elk are down in the valley
in the dried hay field
across from Cedar Hill,

a herd of twenty or more
gathered along the back fence line,
holding their regal brown heads

high on their strong-muscled bodies,
their comical rumps,
white as November snow.

Elk have a way of disappearing;
you see them on one rancher's land
and an hour later, they're gone.

> *Are they lying under*
> *the bare cottonwoods?*
> *Did they migrate down*
> *to drink at the river*
> *behind the red willows?*

Elusive, skittish, elk flee
in a rumble of hoofs
at any human sound or approach

yet they'll let a line of drivers wait
when their twelve-point leader
decides to cross the highway.

Continued

I saw a young one once
fall back each time it tried a fence
it couldn't jump. Suddenly

a great bull ran back across the road
and firmly nudged it with his head
and freed it like God would.

Sunset Horses

dance in a golden field,
their ears held up like feathers,
eyes blue, sometimes green,
and in this new light
I want to change my skin,
ideas about what's possible.

When dusk wind blows,
their manes become flame,
wild grasses catch fire
beneath their bodies, and legs
nearly entwining, they gallop
across purple sky.

For Alice Billings

September Yellow

In the yellow season
rabbit brush grows profuse
and pungent at roadsides,

bouquets of golden eye daisies
reach skyward. Tall sunflowers
lean, black-centered and many-

branched against rail fences.
On hillsides aspen
leaves change to gold,

their light flickering in blue air,
like moths or small flames.
This is a time of dying.

You know that means
you and I will die someday, too—
perhaps with slow aging or

a more certain diminishment
or we could be struck in sunlight
today, sudden as the eagle in flight

seizes the heart of its prey:
I want to believe there's no grief
in this, but a gratitude.

In memory of Carol Rieger

Red Fox

A blaze of gold
          more than red
in early evening light,
          you strode slow through snow-
dusted new grass, skirting
          a low hill behind the house.
Then black ears pointed up, you sensed
          my presence on the porch
and turned your sleek head, sharp nose,
          toward me quick-
flashing black bead eyes.

How you lit up
          the dull afternoon
with your confidence
          and bravado

and in that moment gave me
          a grim hint of your intent
before you trod soundless
          to the forest edge
where lesser creatures live.

Bright hunter—
          what more do I have
to fear or desire?

Geese

Let the land be still
as the windless cottonwoods,
as leaves that cling to oak trees,
copper in morning's pale sun.
Let minds be still,
study the way they hold
to thin branches, giving
cover for small birds.
Let eyes rest on this brilliance.

Let light shine through
the bleached sky backlighting them,
rimming high clouds behind
a flock of Canada geese
who break this silence,
calling out from their flyway
over the peaks, waving
the white flags of their wings.

Transition

The landscape disassembles:
what was sky becomes a frozen pond.
Yarrow, dried pungent and brown,
bends to the hard earth,
cinquefoil yellows and gives up
its store of small coins.
At the feet of the bared trees
blown leaves group and regroup,
black and twisted oaks
stand like mute supplicants
on the hills, wild grasses bow down.

What was filled with sound
grows silent, even the nuthatches
feeding quietly. Listen.
You can hear the earth turning.
You can hear the breaking down of its bones.

Eagle

I was just driving downhill
        when across the quiet creek
I passed the spotted horses
        holding up their blazed heads,
and in the frozen field
        black and white cows
moving like a river
        toward the unrolled hay.
I was just thinking about my luck

when I saw the wintering eagles—
        five sitting in the cottonwoods,
brown bodies stalwart vessels,
        erect heads capped with white
like an anointment.

Suddenly one dove fast to find fish
        in the slow-moving river.
The work of its powerful beak
        was not a thing of particular pride.

Lynx

Out of the aspens and willows
        beside the road, it froze,
wearing gray and white fur.
        A thick-muscled thing,
it came on silent feet, on
        sturdy legs like wound springs.

Are you ever afraid?
        Have you ever feared for your life?

With dark round eyes slit
        it stared at me, full-faced,
pointed ears black tipped,
        hunter's mouth grimaced,

and let me look
        for one moment between us, peace,
then sprang up and disappeared
        into the safety of trees.

Consider

My task is seeing the world—
        today the red coneflower,
        the yellow bee,
        the blue heron
        at the river's edge.

Where else would I go or could I—
        in these plain clothes,
with this boulder for a seat,
        with these eyes?

All day I try to keep my mind on this
        important calling,
the only way I know
        to save the earth.

Love Geology

The Hard Way

See? Over in the wild rye grass?
Mulleins grow like cabbages,
black medic and musk thistles
enough to keep me
weeding every morning in the sun.

I hold my ground on tired knees,
give what I can of thriving space
to Shasta daisies the wind plays with,
to stalks of scented iris,
to the perfect red poppies.

Bent to the task with shiny tools,
I dig, pry, and pull till my hands
grow numb, thumbs blister, bound
to unearth the stubborn, whitish root
of each prostrate clump
of purple-flowering Amaranthaceae.

My husband says *why bother?*
It's all green. You'll lose
the battle anyway.
And well-meaning friends ask *why*
not spray? But something
in me wants to leave a mark
by my own hands in this place
of desert soil and steadfast rock.

Weather at 12,000 Feet

We found the lake called Columbine,
blue glacial bowl, sky-lightened for a time,
and seeing it gave us hope enough

to locate and retrace prints our boots made
almost erased by falling snow.
One of us talked about his recent divorce—

he'd missed signs, too—then hadn't the power
to stop. A rock unloosed goes its own way
until it comes to rest in a new place

such as that high, hummocked basin we crossed,
snow veiling the drab remains of wind-bent
summer flowers as the whole sky turned metallic.

When thunder struck, we dropped our poles
onto the skree, watched pikas flee
to rocky dens, felt hands and faces chill.

We put on every layer in our packs
and, leaning together against one taller crag,
opened up a map to check the route, then

ate a few bites of wet lunch, ice
on the lips of water bottles. Guidebooks say
to pack warm hats, gloves, jackets, socks,

but we don't always stay alert for sudden shifts
or warnings like we saw on the way up—
gropple that was already dropping thick.

Slot Canyon

Ancient waters scoured
these crevices and spirals
in red sandstone I climb
bending my soft body
to fit unyielding curves.

I trust my feet to grip,
arm muscles to pull me
to each higher place.
If I fall, how far?

Where space opens up
wide enough for two,
you grasp and clamber first,
hold your hand to help me,
find us shallow footholds,
sunlight assuring exit
from this labyrinth.

How will we be changed
when we emerge to blue
sky and juniper desert?
Will the world?

The Comfort of Stones

On mesa top their presence calls to me
from under juniper where I seek shade—
stones lying on adobe, dry and dusty,
once waterborne, displaced from riverbed
or muddy bank or Rio Chama flood
before a lake submerged that place of bones,
before the dam when trees and llanos drowned,
unearthed, carried to new repose—these stones,
two small and brown, a third one black and cut
with white like petroglyphs—what a rock knows.
I stoop to gather them, feel their cool weight
tumble in my hand like dice, then close
them in my fist for luck, or for one day,
comfort, when things greater fall away.

On Mount Elbert*

Sun's just past sky center
on this perch of graveled earth,
end point of a long morning

my muscles surmounted gravity
to get me up so high
where wind and sunlight magnify.

I sit, breathe deep,
stretch weary arms and legs,
down shoulders ease my pack
into a shallow shelter

hikers built with boulders,
then pocket for a young child
one small stone.

Far down I mark the path
of my ascent past tree line,
filled bowls of sapphire lakes,

thin ribbons of gray road,
then circle in 360 views,
and reach my fingertips into

this clarity of blue,
farthest space I've ever hiked up to
where all of Colorado slides away.

*Mount Elbert, at 14,433 feet, is the highest mountain in Colorado.

Wild Raspberries

Beside the dusty road
I first see them, red jewels
glittering in green brambles

high up on a steep slope.
My gender's patterned me
to forage like my sister Eve

so I stop the truck and clamber up
to pick the glowing berries.
Who can deny the lure

of wild fruit, sure attraction
of what's unowned and free?
Stickers on bent branches warn me,

but they taste so ripe and delicious;
a few so delicate break apart
before I put them in my mouth.

We thought they might be poisonous.
What are they? Can we eat them?
Smiling, I call down to the young couple,

Yes, yes, these are wild raspberries.
By now I can no longer tell
my blood from their sweet juice

as, guilty, I watch them succumb
on the sunny hill beneath me.
two once perfect also strangers.

Flag Woman

She stands in the middle
of U.S. Highway 550 in a white hard hat,
long sleeves, jeans and dusty work boots.

Blond hair's back in a braid
tied with faded blue bandana,
sunglasses mirror the line of vehicles.

One gloved hand touches the pager
at her waist—it connects her to the crew
working farther up the road.

With the other she holds a red sign
that reads STOP on one side,
SLOW on the reverse.

All day the flag woman holds it up
to signal drivers to stop
or drive slow in the one lane the crew

has repaved or in the one left to do
while inside our vehicles we check watches,
hold cell phones to our ears, turn on air.

We drum fingers on the wheel
with one hand, hover at the gearshift
with the other while she stands

in the hot sun, studies the quiet
white-faced cattle in a nearby field,
brushes loose hair from her tanned face.

Love Geology

One evening we drive down the river road,
red-dusty from a lack of summer rain,
not traveled much this hour after supper.

We've come to search for flagstones
to pave a shady place next to the house we think
we'd like to sit: a friend said he got some

near these high sandstone cliffs
up from the river bank across the road.
Over the years these sedimentaries cleaved

and fell to new repose, half-buried or lodged
near sturdy firs or trunks of knotted gambel oaks.
So you stop the truck when I say

There and *Over there*
so I can scramble up through brush
when we spot one, or two a little further up.

Then I push them down to you, or you climb
up the steeper banks, worried I might fall.
The stones you lower down the slope to me

I lift in my scratched hands and
with slow care stack in the truck.
Each heavy, red-brown slab I hold

an earth gift: I, the thrifty one,
always wanting to make something
out of what's free I can find,

you, the one who bears the heavy burden
to content me, who says if I want,
you'd move a mountain.

Bear Story

A bear visited the porch late in the night.
We heard the crash and frantic work it was
up to before we saw its shadowy bulk,

dark-furred body through the dim window.
We thought it sought balmy water in
the hot tub, covered tight as a drum,

but it was acorns underneath a redwood
corner lured it, hid by a squirrel.
Hungry and adept, it broke wood slats,

tossed insulating foam into the yard,
then ate its fill of those secreted seeds.
Daylight revealed to us bear paw prints,

and though we think we're safe behind a wall,
we know a beast was in the garden
by the damage done. This was a feast and run.

Climbing Utah

You can never know the position of an object
if you know its energy. You cannot know its
energy if you know its position.
                    Werner Heisenberg

Held in by cerulean sky,
          tethered by fragrant, ragged junipers,
                    these ancient rocks know
                              the effort of remaining in one place.
Shapes time and wind carved
          some see an animal or window,
                    others famous avenue or cathedral
and measured against their buttresses,
          I'm a small Gulliver woman.

Like a novice sailor, I climb
          fins resembling ships or whales,
                    great blood-red monoliths,
time-weathered smooth
          or ridged or pock-marked
                    as the skin of a humpback.
My hands labor to find grip,
          toes small holes in their steep flanks.
For me, work's a certainty~
          I sweat, stretch leg muscles,
                    a reluctant explorer.

At each new rock mass
          I guess at the energy leashed inside~
                    What formula could be written?

If these stones could move, where would they go?
          What would they say if they could speak?

Remembering the Himalayas

Five yaks live in a field across the road
        my neighbor owns. They pasture there
or rest inside a wooden shed
        he built for them for snow and cold.

Great black and white-haired beasts, they singly walk
        the field south, then back north, bearing their weight
over wide swaths they cut in summer grass,
        fetlocks swaying, horned heads bowing down.

I think they are remembering the Himalayas
        they climbed with heavy panniers of grain
skeins of their soft wool were traded for
        women loomed in low-roofed winter rooms:

I want to travel where their walking leads—
        in one dark eye's a mirror to that place—
to hear their hoof beats echoing on stone,
        the plaintive sound of far-off village bells.

Traditions

Under a Madonna's robe sky
      men are cutting hay on hillsides
beneath the Dolomiti crags, honey-colored
      or white gleaming, towering
beyond the tall and dark fir forest.
      Laboring in summer's sun, they
gather it with rakes into small trucks
      that somehow keep upright on the steep slopes.

Still higher the Putea and Kreutspitze
      hold us for a day in their green
valley where shadows deepen
      as we descend the stony path
back into town where at this hour
      women in aprons or jeans
carry pails of water to flowers
      in the cemetery—geraniums,
blue lobelia, marigolds— and in that garden
      of iron crosses, stand or kneel.

How these acts are passed down.
      We wonder if we have
any tradition of our own,
      we the visitors with our polite English,
they with their German or Italian
      who smile at us as they cross
the street from the church
      while we photograph each other
in front of its carved, ancient door.

Chanterelles

Up in the pines near fallen logs
we find them clustered, heaved up through
needled earth, or under leaves,
bright yellow, and if we look close,
with scalloped caps like lilies have.

A little song to frighten ghosts?
Late summer dance around a tree?
Two days after thunderstorms
mycophagists have no fears to fend.

I gather them from soft, black beds
cutting at each moss-buried base,
then place them gently in a bag
to take home. I can almost taste
the buttery dish they'll make for us
adventurous, sometime-gourmets.
Their gold rubs off on my fingers.

Burning

No wind means a good day to burn the brush
stacks that grew all summer by the road
when we pruned piñons or oaks or barrowed a load
of weeds. The morning's chill and hush—
heavy November sky gray as the smoke
that rises when your bare hand flares the match.
I touch what's dried or gone to seed and watch
each branch and blade of grass ignite you stoke.

As flames leap fragrant wood and brittle leaves,
I see future and past, this end-of-year
ritual transforming what was alive to air.
Like moths, white ash ascends from our small griefs
that smolder in the heap—their presence here
proves we survive to feed each other's fire.

Mallards

November mutes the river sounds
     and walkers dwindle to a few—
along the path cattails and autumn
     sage are brown and gray, their scents
mingle with leaves of cottonwoods.

Sun no longer high, dun hills
     extend to meet a dimmer sky
patched with blue, and how I praise
     this calm of subtle color, hush
of summer's noise and blaze. Only

heart beats, footfalls, my breathing in
     say I'm alive and not dreaming.
I'll find a haven with my love—
     to shelter in the thin, dried weeds
a pair of shining mallards skims,
     crossing a green and rippled pond.

Shoulder Season

Signs on shop doors read
Open weekends only
See you at Thanksgiving
Closing at 6:00 p.m.
It's the time of year
when the body of tourists
shrugs away from Main Street,
when the strong arms of merchants
take a temporary rest.

Gray and golden, the days grow shorter,
begin and end in shadow,
and the white-topped mountains
draw their cloaks around town
like ragged scarecrows or ghosts.

We locals can find parking places
on any street and traffic wanes
on Highway 550. At the roadside
deer stand watching us in familiar groups.

Inside our houses, we sigh deep,
breathe slower, read thicker books
and try out recipes for soup
we simmer on little-used back burners.
Down our backs the weight
of the year begins to ease.

The Color of Snow

Vermeer asked the maid
What color are clouds?
And he wouldn't take white
for an answer. She looked
hard at the Delft sky,
then slow replied
yellow and *green....red!*

In snow I see red, too,
on my way down from Miller Mesa.
I've been snowshoeing,
soft slapping and crunching
what's new fallen,
all afternoon following
winter-transformed trails
through untouched meadows,
hushed forest of laden pines
and naked aspens, leaving
a giant's deep tracks.

Now the sky's lavender
and the distant peaks
I try to name violet
as late sun paints shadows
on boulders and drifts,
broad brushstrokes
over a canvas of foothills,
sometimes blue and *yes* green.

Moon, Trees, Snow

Ironton's still as ghosts and cold
     when we fast ski a trail laid down
by miners in this high valley
     where snow's deep filled the ground.

From the starred sky a disc of moon
     guides our way, spreading light
where fir and pine trees stand
     now like ghosts draped in white
and meadows glitter more than gold.

Underneath the tree-snagged moon
     there's silence all the woods around
except a stream's rippling sound.
     Not speaking in the calm and chill,
we hear only the squeak and crunch
     of skis on snow, reach and glide
the rhythm of our thoughts.

Back at the trail start six does stand
     in the headlights of the car,
watchful eyes reflecting moons,
     wordless, breaths warming the air.

Looking Back

From the room's shade
      narrow oak trunks,
          black, twist
around birds at varying heights
      who call the morning,
all their notes marked with
      the eagerness of news reporters.

Sounds of sporadic vehicles
      near, far, then silent
fill the air, carry
      the moment to the ear.

Calm comes
      by raising the eye
to dawn-lit peaks
      lined up against sky
in their familiar patterns.

My sons would be
      at ease here
as they were all the summer days
      we lived around a blue pool

and my parents would be smiling
      as if they never divorced
before they grew old and one died,

even myself
      younger face unlined,
          eyes clear, mind full
of what it's no longer filled with.

Instead it is this moment,
      black channeled, branched,
          my fingers touching bark.

About the Author

Beth Paulson teaches writing and creativity workshops in Ouray County, Colorado where she has lived since 1999. She taught English at California State University Los Angeles for more than twenty years. She is the author of two previous poetry collections, *The Truth About Thunder* (2001) and *The Company of Trees* (2004). Her poems have appeared widely in literary magazines and national  anthologies, and her work was nominated for the Pushcart Prizes for 2007 and 2009.

Printed in the United States
150085LV00001B/49/P